INVISIBLE IDOL

PART I

Ernest Jeffry

Copyright © 2016 Ernest Jeffry

Cover Design by Ernest Jeffry

Contents

Introduction

First Invisible Idol

What happens after getting the High Position?

Is it rightful to expect for High Position?

Why it is not right to expect for High Position?

Where do People expect High Position?

Conclusion

Bibliography

About the Author

Special Thanks

Chapter-I Introduction

Genesis 17:1 "....I am the Almighty God; walk before me, and be thou perfect." God is Almighty.

Christ the Son of God(Matthew 3: 17, Matthew 16:16, John 1:49) was praised by the holy angels in Heaven. Isaiah 14: 12 ".... Lucifer, son of the morning!....." One of the most beautiful creation of God and the chief of Angels who sang praises to God was Lucifer.

God the Father, Son and Holy Ghost, the Trinity-Matthew 28:19 "....the name of the Father, and of the Son, and of the Holy Ghost:", who are one in three persons are praised all the time. God is greatly to be praised.

Genesis 2:4 "These are the generations of the heavens and of the earth when they were created, in the day that the Lord God made the earth and the heavens." God formed the universe and all that is therein.

Every living thing should only worship God. He is in the highest place where human beings can't reach in Human form.

Exodus 19:21 "And the Lord said unto Moses, Go down, charge the people, lest they break through unto the Lord to gaze, and many of them perish" Exodus 33: 20 "And he said, Thou canst not see my face: for there shall no man see me, and live." God is so powerful that sinful human beings will be burnt to ashes in the presence of God.

Exodus 33:11 "And the Lord spake unto Moses face to face, as a man speaketh unto his friend...." Exodus 33: 21-23 " And the Lord said, Behold, there is a place by me, and thou shalt stand upon a rock: And it shall come to pass, while my glory passeth by, that I will put thee in a clift of the rock, and will cover thee with my hand while I pass by: And I will take away mine hand, and thou shalt see my back parts: but my face shall not be seen." Moses was the only person who survived when he saw the back of the almighty when he passed by quickly.

Man is the only creation of God who was given the power to discern good and evil. In the Garden of Eden, our first parents were educated to know that which was good.

Lucifer, who become Satan, tempted the woman to disobey God's command. Isaiah14: 13 & 14 "For thou hast said in thine heart, I will ascend into heaven, I will exalt my throne above the stars of God: I will sit also upon the mount of the congregation, in the sides of the north: I will ascend above the heights of the clouds; I will be like the most High." Lucifer, who was next to the God heads wanted to step-up to a position above Son of God.

Love of HIGHEST POSITION led to the fall of Lucifer. Lucifer wanted to become God. His thoughts deviated from praising God. Day by day his anxiety grew more to become God.

Isaiah 14: 12 "How thou art fallen from heaven, O Lucifer,..." When this was understood by God, he was thrown out of Heaven and he landed on earth. He took the form of a serpent to deceive woman.

Physical materials or thoughts that take precedence over God are considered to be an Idol. The Bible clearly says in the book of Exodus 20: 3 & 4. Verse 3 "Thou shalt have no other Gods before me."

Verse 4 "Thou shalt not make unto thee any graven image, or any likeness of any thing that is in heaven above, or that is in the earth beneath, or that is in the water under the earth:"

Verse 5 "Thou shalt not bow down thyself to them, nor serve them: for I the Lord thy God am a jealous God, visiting the iniquity of the fathers upon the children unto the third and fourth generation of them that hate me;"

Verse 4 gives a clear definition of the graven images that is physical Idols. There are other idols that rule our thoughts over God. We'll see each of the idols in the upcoming series of this book.

Chapter-II First Invisible Idol

One of the most loved idol ruling people, nowadays, is the first thought that Lucifer had in heaven. Get a high position in their organization or place of worship or locality.

People's thoughts and focus are fixed on this idol which ruins the relationship with God. Most of their time is wasted on thoughts of obtaining the top designation that they desperately want in the workplace.

This idol when it creeps into the mind is like cancer which keeps growing day by day without any symptoms. When it matures, it disrupts the entire system and collapses the person.

Let's take few men from the Holy Bible who were made great.

Genesis 12:1 & 2 " Now the Lord had said unto Abram, Get thee out of thy country, and from thy kindred, and from thy father's house, unto a land that I will shew thee: And I will make thee a great nation, and I will bless thee, and make thy name great; and thou shalt be a blessing;"

Abraham didn't know that he would be called Father of Faith. He was unaware of true God. But when he heard his voice to move out of his home country to the place that God showed, he started without any hesitation. He was made a big nation.

Further in the book of Genesis, we read Joseph was God

fearing and followed God's precepts perfectly. He was revealed in many dreams that he will rule over his brothers. Genesis 37: 7-11 "For, behold, we were binding sheaves in the field, and lo, my sheaf arose, and also stood upright; and, behold, your sheaves stood round about, and made obeisance to my sheaf. And his brethren said to him, Shalt thou indeed reign over us?

Or shalt thou indeed have dominion over us? And they hated him yet the more for his dreams, and for his words. And he dreamed yet another dream, and told it his brethren, and said, Behlod, I have dreamed a dream more; and, behold, the sun and the moon and the eleven stars made obeisance to me. And he told it to his father, and to his brethren: and his father rebuked him, and said unto him, what is this dream that thou hast dreamed?

Shall I and thy mother and thy brethren indeed come to bow down ourselves to thee to the earth?

And his brethren envied him; but his father observed the saying"

This shows how the high position has created anger and jealously among own brothers that led them to hurt their own brother and sell him as a slave to a faraway land.

In Genesis 37: 36 "And the Midianites sold him into Egypt unto Potiphar, an officer of Pharaoh's, and captain of the guard." Who was sold to Potiphar?

Genesis 41: 38-43 "And Pharaoh said unto his servants, can we find such a one as this is, a man in whom the spirit of God is?

And Pharaoh said unto Joseph, Forasmuch as God hath shewed thee all this, there is non so discreet and wise as thou art: Thou shalt be over my house, and according unto thy word shall all my people be ruled: only in the throne will I be greater than thou. And Pharaoh said unto Joseph, See, I have set thee over all the land of Egypt.

And Pharaoh took off his ring from his hand, and put it upon Joseph's hand, and arrayed him in vestures of fine linen, and put a gold chain about his neck; And he made him to ride in the second chariot which he had; and they cried before him, Bow the knee: and he made him ruler over all the land of Egypt"

Joseph was brought as a slave to Egypt, in nowise he knew that he will be made next to the king of Egypt. If Joseph anticipated to become next to the King of Egypt and forgot God, could he himself been able to reach that position?

Joseph followed the commandments of God diligently that was taught by his beloved father. He was tempted and tried but he stood firm in the faith and let God work His plan through him.

He was made next to King of an ungodly nation and he was permitted to worship the true living God by the heathen King.

People, should wait on the Lord to work in them. Tell their wishes and needs to God in prayer, even though he knows it before they ask Him.

The worldly designation and position is temporary. We will not carry it into heaven.

David the shepherd boy, beloved of God, was taking care of his sheep. Did he imagine that he will rule a great nation?

David had fullest faith in God and was able to single handedly kill a lion and a bear. He was wandering on the mountainside grazing and showing water to the sheep.

When it was the right time, God anointed him to be king of Israelites, I Samuel 16:1 – 13 "And the Lord said unto Samuel, How long wilt thou mourn for Saul, seeing I have rejected him from reigning over Israel? fill thine horn with oil, and go, I will send thee to Jesse the Bethlehemite: for I have provided me a king among his sons. And Samuel said, How can I go? If Saul hear it, he will kill me. And the Lord said, Take an heifer with thee, and say, I am come to sacrifice to the Lord. And call Jesse to the sacrifice, and I will shew thee what thou shalt do: and thou shalt anoint unto me him whom I name unto thee.

And Samuel did that which the Lord spake, and came to Beth-lehem. And the elders of the town trembled at this coming, and said, Comest thou peaceable? And he said, Peaceably: I am come to sacrifice unto the Lord: sanctify yourselves, and come with me to the sacrifice.

And he sanctified Jesse and his sons, and called them to the sacrifice. And it came to pass, when they were come, that he looked on Eliab, and said, Surely the Lord's anointed is before him. But the Lord said unto Samuel, Look not on his countenance, or on the height of his stature; because I have refused him: for the Lord seeth not as man seeth; for man looketh on the outward appearance, but the Lord looketh on the heart. Then Jesse called Abinadab, and made him pass before Samuel. And he said, Neither hath the Lord chosen this. Then Jesse made Shammah to pass by. And he said, Neither hath the Lord chosen this. Again, Jesse made seven of his sons to pass before Samuel. And Samuel said unto Jesse. The Lord hath not chosen these. And Samuel said unto Jesee, Are here all thy children? And he said, There remaineth yet the youngest, and behold, he keepeth the sheep. And Samuel said unto Jesse, Send and fetch him:

for we will not sit down till he come hither. And he sent, and brought him in. Now he was ruddy, and withal of a beautiful countenance, and goodly to look to. And the Lord said, Arise, anoint him: for this is he. Then Samuel took the horn of oil, and anointed him in the midst of his brethren: and the Spirit of the Lord came upon David from that day forward. He was selected by God to be the next King of Israel even before he proved his valor. God made him to visit his brothers in the war zone against the Philistines. Without any heavy armor, he was able to win over the Giant.

We may feel that we are very strong, wise in our own sight and can face any situation without God and with human support.

But David and Joseph didn't have an army. Except the support of God, they didn't depend on anyone and expect the big position.

Its the unpreparedness and unwillingness of us to keep God first in all we do that ends up in anxiety, pain, problems and panic attacks.

Chapter –III What happens after getting the high position?

Saul the first human king of Israelites broke all commandments of God. First, Saul attempted to murder David. Then he went in search of strange Gods. Ultimately, he became corrupt.

Absalom wanted to be the next King after his father. For this reason, he sent spies to all the tribes of Israel, to shout when the trumpet blew that he was the King of Hebron. He went on to consult with his army men to create a plot to kill his own father. But in the end he lost his life at a very young age.

In the history of the world, lots of assassination events have happened. When root cause for the events are analyzed, most of the events were to capture the assassinated person's designation

The Bible clearly states the heads of the Sanhedrin of Jesus time were scared that the people might leave them and start following Jesus Christ and their will become powerless. They were behind him to find fault with his teachings and practice. They named his miracles as work of demons. They conspired against him in high places.

They created stories that he was forming a group against the Roman Empire and caused them to crucify him.

People tend to maintain the position and want to move to the next higher designation in their job. Some become insecure and wild to hold on to the designation. They consider it higher than God.

Slowly, their thoughts deviate from God and they spend more time on things that are worldly. Their imagination will go to the extremes to spoil others opportunity to safeguard their designation.

In this wicked world, people join hands to spoil others' opportunities and enjoy the benefits of the unfortunate's spoil.

Some people sell their virginity or have immoral relationship to secure or maintain high position, breaking the commandments of God.

Few hire hooligans to manhandle people whom they consider as competitors for a top position. Day by day wickedness keeps increasing and they fall prey to satan's trap.

These are animal behaviors. In the wild, animals fight within its own species to show their supremacy. It will be watched by their own species and also by other species. When a wild animal makes a kill, there are lots of partakers of the spoil. From the fresh meat till it gets rotten, some steal the spoil, some are scavengers that clear the leftover.

The respect, power, money, etc.., that people receive when they secured a higher designation drives them insane.They feel they have become God and when their sub-ordinates respect them, they feel they are worshiped.

When the high position is achieved, they are praised and flattered. People forget that they should do all for the glory of God. They are carried away by the appreciative words. They love to be praised.

Money is spent in an extra-ordinary manner to sustain in the position. The amount of money that is spent is very huge. This money could have been used for the poor, needy, physically or mentally challenged. But it is wasted for self-glory and supremacy.

It happens, sometimes, that few people who don't deserve the position are appointed for certain roles. They don't know how to handle the office they hold. So, they ill-treat their sub-ordinates. Such behavior is unacceptable to God.

Chapter-IV Is it rightful to expect for high positions?

In the Bible, if you see, Joseph, David, Daniel and all the faithful men have not imagined or expected high posts. Joseph and Daniel were given the opportunity in a foreign land without the supervision of the king.

The heathen kings had full trust in God's men. Since they were faithful to God, they were able to reflect the same character in all their activities.

Sincerity has become their habit.

The Bible says in Luke 16:10 "He that is faithful in that which is least is faithful also in much: and he that is unjust in the least is unjust also in much"

In the parable of talents, where three persons were given different measures of talents. The persons with 5 and 2 talents increased their talents with what was provided but the person with 1 talent buried it and did not make use of it. So the lord who gave those talents returned to see who these three persons were doing. He appreciates the 2 persons who have doubled the talents in Matthew 25: 21 & 23 "His lord said unto him, Well done, thou good and faithful servant: thou hast been faithful over a few things, I will make thee ruler over many things: enter thou into the joy of thy lord"

Habit is formed based on the activities that are performed

repeatedly on a daily basis. For example, a person who wakes up in the morning at 6 o'clock every day, slowly it becomes his habit to wake up at the same time.

It is not right to expect high position until given by God. People strive to get the high position but God's thoughts are different.

Chapter-V Why it is not right to expect High Position?

People who expect high position may not have the right skills to perform/execute the task rather than they try to survive on subordinate's efforts or find faults on others.

The expectation of high position will start to grow big in the mind. When this intention has crept into a person's mind, they start imagining how they will perform the task without knowing about it, act as a boss, change their attitude.

Now the imagination becomes an important part of their lives. Day in and day out, they start worshiping this idol. They forget to worship the true God. Their mind is preoccupied with only this IDOL, High Position or Designation. Priorities in their life will change. All they chant as holy words is the designation. Hence, it's not right to expect for high positions.

They sacrifice their time, energy, thoughts, family relationships, friends, money, and at last God also to obtain high positions. After obtaining the position, they still have to utilize more of their time, energy, thoughts, money to sustain in that position and and move further up. At the end, God is lost in their live.

Sometimes, it's the will of God to permit an incapable person, to take charge of a particular designation. He may be considered as incapable in man's sight but its not the same in God's sight. The Bible says "….for the Lord seeth not as man seeth; for man looketh on the outward appearance, but the Lord looketh on the heart"

In the Bible, we read that God's people were allowed to be captives of heathen kings. God permitted it to happen because their deeds and secret sins kindled the anger of God. When our way of life is not acceptable to God or in line with God's commandments, we become ineligible for the grace and blessings of the Lord. When our personal way of life is not correct, how can the person make a good administrator? Is it right to desire for high position with such attitude?

In such situations, God permits but not out of His control, some evil persons to that the high position or designation.

Its an indicator for us to correct our mistakes. But mostly people tend to blame God for not answering their prayers or say its fate or get depressed and worry.

Until we mend our way of life to be in tune with the living God's commandments. It is not right to expect high position or designation.

God allows trouble to the extent that an individual can handle. God has a purpose in everyone's life. In most instances, there will be only one position for which many people will be contesting but there can be one person for the position. God decides who it should be for the position. Contesting for a position in the fear of God and right spirit without harming anyone in thoughts or deeds is fine, until we get a clear picture of God's plan. In the examples of God's people that we read earlier, God sent people or brought the right person at the right time for a particular position at the appointed time which the right person was unaware. So it is not right to expect high position. We can pray to God to prepare us for such position but if that's not God's purpose in our life, we should be ready to accept it and continue. We should be ready to accept it and continue life's journey without greed, jealous or anger.

Chapter-VI Where do People expect high positions?

Lucifer expected position in the most holy place in the entire universe, the palace of the true living God. Similarly, people want high positions at the place of worship. Firstly, People form groups to target the sincere believers and throw them out of office and settle down in their position.Some hire local gangsters before elections to threaten the deserving humble members. They will be ready to shed blood of the innocent. They trust in the strength of men.

But the Bible clearly states that the strength of men are vain and that whoever depends on human strength will definitely fail.

Secondly, they try to expect high position in workplace. Promotions will automatically reach us when we are sincere, complete our tasks on time and obey the orders. This habit will develop as a character when we are sincere to God.

Thirdly, supremacy amongst relatives. When high positions in office is obtained, people tend to show the same powers within the family and relatives.This will ultimately hammer the family bonding. Over the years people tend to forget their relatives and cling on to new friends or colleagues who are of the same designation or above.

This stage is mentioned in the Bible as "Love will wax cold".

Thirdly, when a group of friends cordially live together, Satan attempts to break the good relationship. The easiest weapon will be to trick one among the group to create a sub group within themselves to disturb the harmony

We would have heard and learned in the history of the world that few leaders were assassinated to get control of their positions

This IDOL is INVISIBLE and grows within a person in their mind. People are unable to visualize it.

Satan takes full control over such individuals who yield themselves willfully. People don't realize they are committing sin and this is the idol they worship sincerely and without fail all throughout their life time. This Idol does not belong to religion, caste or tribe. But worshiped by most of the human beings.

This Idol worship leads them to a dangerous end. Every person has been created for a purpose on this earth. Ask God to reveal the purpose of your life and fulfill it for the glory of God. God has given the power of choice to choose between good and evil. It is in the hand of the individual to make the right choice.

Chapter-VII Conclusion

The Ten Commandments clearly states, "Thou shalt have no other Gods before me"

Let God speak in your heart to differentiate God and Idol worship

"Let every thing that has breath praise the Lord. Praise ye the Lord" - Psalms 150:6

Bibliography

King James Version Bible

About the Author

Ernest Jeffry is a post graduate in Management with vast experience in corporate world. In his roles of Lecturer and Corporate Trainer, he has worked with people of different culture across the globe.

He is a traveller and travel blogger. He is interested in latest technology and science. He has found that people are depressed, sad and worried about something. His aspiration to find simple solution for people's depression led to this series of books. His creativity and counselling has helped many people find happiness.

Special Thanks

A special thanks to my parents Mr. Selvaraj and Mrs. Heys Ratnam for teaching me the Bible. They have helped to review the book and my wife, Noreen Rao, too.

Invisible Idol Series

This is the first of the series of upcoming Invisible Idols, a religious psychology book.